BIBLICAL MARRIAGE: A CONCISE
RESOURCE FOR CHRISTIAN COUPLES
PREPARING FOR MARRIAGE

BIBLICAL Marriage:

A CONCISE RESOURCE FOR CHRISTIAN COUPLES PREPARING FOR MARRIAGE

BENJAMIN & LAUREN HUTSON
STEPHEN & MANDY VIPPERMAN

Charleston, SC
www.PalmettoPublishing.com

Biblical Marriage
Copyright © 2023 by
Benjamin & Lauren Hutson
Stephen & Mandy Vipperman

All rights reserved

No portion of this book may be reproduced, stored in a retrieval system, or transmitted in any form by any means–electronic, mechanical, photocopy, recording, or other–except for brief quotations in printed reviews, without prior permission of the author.

First Edition

Paperback ISBN: 979-8-8229-0078-3
eBook ISBN: 979-8-8229-0079-0

Benjamin and Stephen *would like to dedicate* this book to our wonderful and godly wives with deepest gratitude for their long-suffering nature as we strive to be the husbands that God calls us to be.

TABLE OF CONTENTS

Preface ix

Chapter 1: Purpose of Marriage 1

Chapter 2: Leaving and Cleaving 7

Chapter 3: Covenant, Not Contract...................... 12

Chapter 4: Equally Yoked 20

Chapter 5: Leadership and Love......................... 28

Chapter 6: Sex Matters.................................. 36

Chapter 7: Pornography................................ 43

Chapter 8: Communication Matters..................... 48

Chapter 9: Prayer Matters 55

Chapter 10: Money Matters............................. 61

Chapter 11: Church Matters............................. 68

Chapter 12: Conclusion................................. 78

About the Authors..................................... 81

PREFACE

This book is intended for Christians intending to unite in marriage or those who want to understand what the Bible says about this God-designed institution. Those who reject the teachings of the Bible will most likely not agree with the majority of what is written in this book. A wise man once said, "There is a way that seems right to a man, but in the end, it leads to death" (Prov. 14:12, NIV). This book is not about what seems right. This book is about what God has designed and declared marriage to be.

This book employs many Scriptural verses about marriage. We intend to state the biblical matters plainly and without apology. Many of these biblical principles will be offensive to non-Christians. However, we believe following Christ is act an of willing submission to Christ and his Word. You do not have to believe the Bible if you do not want to believe the Bible. You are free to reject the Word of God and the values of God to embrace the value system of the world, but that decision comes with consequences.

Before you do that, we would like you to consider something. If the world is so wise, then why is the divorce rate so high? Is it because married couples are fully embracing God's design for marriage or because they have rejected God's plan? This book is based on the fundamental fact that God knows the perfect recipe for marriage.

If you have not trusted in Christ and submitted to his Lordship, and you continue to read this book, it might make you angry. However, please understand that your anger is directed toward the God who created you and the God who created the institution of marriage.

Jesus said you cannot put new wine into old wineskins; doing so destroys both. Such would be the case if a non-Christian tried to implement these Christian values without first surrendering to the Lordship of Jesus. Christianity is not something you add to your life as you might add a new item to a collection. When you become a Christian, God transforms your whole life. Without that divine transformation, you are not capable of appreciating the biblical values explained in this book. We encourage you to repent of your sin and surrender to the Lordship of Jesus Christ. Then we believe you can understand and practice the marriage principles of this book.

The perfect marriage advice is for you and your spouse to strive to be sinless. Sin is the cause of every problem in every relationship. Sinlessness is a very high goal to set—perhaps so high that it discourages you from trying to attain it. However, as believers, we have been called to pursue holiness because the God we serve is holy.

As believers in Jesus and as those who have the Holy Spirit dwelling within us, we understand that we still battle the flesh. Perfect sinlessness in this life is something we believe is the goal, but in this life, we will not reach sinless

perfection because of our fallen state. With that in mind, Larry Christenson offers the perfect marriage advice with a goal that is attainable:

The secret of good family life is disarmingly simple: Cultivate the family's relationship with Jesus Christ.[1]

If you are a Christian who believes the Bible is the Word of God, but you have had trouble finding verses about marriage, then this book is for you. God's Word will expose your shortcomings as a husband or wife and challenge you to be transformed according to the wisdom of God.

> For the word of God is living and active. Sharper than any double-edged sword, it penetrates even to dividing soul and spirit, joints and marrow; it judges the thoughts and attitudes of the heart.
> **—Hebrews 4:12 (NIV)**

We create significant problems when we are not the husband or wife God has designed us to be. Many products come with a warning label: "Use only as intended by the manufacturer." Such is the case with marriage. Your marriage should follow the guidelines set forth by God, for he is the Architect, Creator, and Sustainer of your life. When you try to make a square peg fit in a round hole, you damage both. When you use carnal solutions to resolve spiritual

---

1 Larry Christenson, *The Christian Family* (Minneapolis: Bethany Fellowship, 1970), p. 14.

problems, you cause more problems. Sin has consequences. The biblical solutions for sin are confession and repentance and trusting in the finished work of the Sinless Savior. When you fall short of the biblical standard, acknowledge that and repent. Be the husband or wife God intends for you to be so that you do not damage yourself and your marriage.

Battle of the Sexes

Have you ever wondered when the battle of the sexes began? Sadly, it began with the first man and woman, Adam and Eve. When Adam and Eve sinned, God listed out the consequences of that sin in Genesis 3:14–19. In 3:16 (NIV), God said to the woman:

> Your desire will be for your husband,
> and he will rule over you.

It sounds lovely that the wife would desire her husband, but unfortunately, something has been lost in translation. In the original Hebrew language, that exact phrase is found in Genesis 4:7 (NIV), when God warns Cain that sin is crouching at his door: "It desires to have you, but you must master it." The translation of Genesis 4:7 does a much better job of capturing the adversarial relationship embedded in the same Hebrew phrase found in Genesis 3:16. It indicates an adversarial relationship between man and woman. The wife will desire to rule over the husband just as sin desires

to rule over the soul, but God has granted authority to the husband. That is how the battle of the sexes began.

Every wife will challenge the authority of her husband, but to what extent? Some wives will be relentless. Other wives will challenge their husbands while hoping their husbands will stand up straight and not yield their authority. Some wives think this battle is win or lose; if he wins, then she loses. Truthfully, if the husband caves to pressure and yields his authority, they both lose.

A Marriage Story
Comparing your life to the biblical standard can be discouraging as you realize that you have sinned and fallen short of the glory of God. You need to be aware of your shortcomings and committed to biblical standards, but we do not want you to be discouraged. The following story relates the marriage of one of the worst husbands and worst wives ever. Whatever your shortcomings may be, be encouraged; you are doing better than these two.

There once was a king who was given authority to rule over God's chosen people. His name was Ahab, and he needed a wife. Many kings would marry the princess of a neighboring kingdom. Such marriages helped forge treaties. However, God's people were not allowed to marry foreign women, not because they were of a different race but because they were of a different faith.

Ahab did not care what God wanted. He married the foreigner Jezebel. Jezebel was relentless in challenging the authority of her husband. Ahab was weak. He did not have a strong relationship with God, so he did not know how to lead properly. Thus, Jezebel, a pagan woman, ruled the kingdom of Israel.

Jezebel did not allow the Israelites to worship God. Instead, she made them worship Baal. She killed as many prophets of God as she could and made sure the prophets of Baal were well supplied.

One day, a great and powerful prophet of God named Elijah called for a showdown on Mount Carmel. King Ahab and 450 prophets of Baal were all invited to the contest. Elijah called down fire from heaven, and then he went on a killing rampage, slaughtering the 450 prophets of Baal. King Ahab witnessed the power of God in the man of God, but Elijah was not finished. Elijah told the king that the three-year drought was over and that heavy rains were coming. He told the king that he had better hitch up his chariot, because if the king tarried, his chariot would get stuck in the mud. Then Elijah laced up his sandals and outran the king's chariot!

After such an incredible display of the power of God, you would think that Ahab's spine would be stiffened, and he would be ready to take back power from his wife. Unfortunately, Jezebel crushed any notion Ahab might have had of leading the kingdom. She immediately ordered the execution of Elijah, but she was unsuccessful in killing him.

Sometime later King Ahab was sulking like a child when Jezebel came to see him. Ahab whined to his wife like a child. He explained that he had tried to acquire Naboth's vineyard but failed. She coddled him the way a mother would a toddler and then used the king's royal seal to write orders ensuring that Naboth would be murdered.

This couple epitomizes the exact opposite of what God intends in marriage. The husband should not act like a child. The wife should not rule over the husband. It did not end well for Ahab and Jezebel; see 1 Kings 16:29–22:40 and 2 Kings 9–10.

To a greater or lesser extent, every man has the weakness of Ahab. There are times when he wants to quit and times when he wants to lay down the burden of leadership.

To a greater or lesser extent, every woman has the spirit of Jezebel. Every woman will challenge her husband's authority. God has said as much in Genesis 3:16. A full-blooded Jezebel rejoices in her husband's abdication of responsibility.

The godly woman says, "Don't yield your leadership! We may challenge you and your authority, but in the recesses of our hearts, we want you to win. You must win!"[2]

---

[2] Christenson, p. 135, my paraphrase.

The husband who is a full-blooded Ahab will not be loved and respected. He will be despised. His wife will become bitter and resentful of his laziness in leadership.

The godly husband will not be lazy in leadership. He will work hard to make sure his family draws close to Jesus. His wife may challenge him from time to time, but she will also respect him, knowing that if she follows him, they will grow closer to Jesus and closer together.

CHAPTER 1:
Purpose of Marriage

The relationship between husband and wife is very important to God. Man and woman were created in the very first chapter of the first book of the Bible. They are the crowning achievement of God's creative work and the only part of creation made in God's image. This relationship deserves our utmost attention.

Among other lessons, Genesis 2 offers us insight into the purpose of marriage. ***God says it is not good for man to be alone.*** It is the first thing that God identifies as not good. Up to this point, everything has been called good. Thus, it is a significant statement about the purpose of marriage.

Loneliness is a devastating force. We are made in the image of the triune God (Father, Son, and Holy Spirit), who has never been alone. We are made with an intrinsic desire to have relationships, and the most intimate relationship a person can have with another human being is found in marriage.

> He who finds a wife finds what is good and receives favor from the LORD.
> **—Proverbs 18:22 (NIV)**

Human beings are social creatures. Everyone needs an intimate relationship with another human being. It is incredibly important and will have a major impact on your spiritual, physical, emotional, and mental health.

Gary Smalley and John Trent have written an excellent parenting book, *The Gift of the Blessing*, which includes some heartbreaking stories of children who have suffered from parents who did not know how to love and bless them.[3] The impacts on those children living in the absence of a loving relationship are devastating. ***Ideally, you should have learned how to love your spouse through the love you received from your parents and by observing your parents and how they loved each other.*** If you did not grow up with loving parents, you are going to have much to learn and much to overcome to have a biblical marriage.

> **Companionship doubles the joy.**

COMPANIONSHIP MEANS DOUBLING the joy and dividing the sorrows. There is a joke about a preacher who takes a sick day, but he skips church to get in a round of golf. The preacher makes a hole in one but is extremely exasperated because he cannot tell anyone about it. Companionship doubles the joy. It is an awful thing to have some achievement worth celebrating and no one to celebrate with you.

---

3 Gary Smalley and John Trent, *The Gift of the Blessing* (Nashville: Thomas Nelson, 1993), pp. 118–150.

That kind of loneliness leads to despair that, in some ways, is worse than having no one to help divide the sorrows. That kind of loneliness often causes people to give up. After all, what is the point of achievement if no loved one can bear witness to your hard-earned accomplishment? It is the sadness of shouting into an empty canyon and knowing only you will hear the echo.

> **Companionship divides the sorrow.**

HAVING A LOVED one to help divide the sorrow is also important.

> Two are better than one, because they have a good return for their work: If one falls down, his friend can help him up. But pity the man who falls and has no one to help him up! Also, if two lie down together, they will keep warm. But how can one keep warm alone? Though one may be overpowered, two can defend themselves. A cord of three strands is not quickly broken.
> **—Ecclesiastes 4:9–12 (NIV)**

Some people who fall short of the biblical standard will often rise to the challenge when their spouses fall ill or face tragedy. The need of the spouse awakens a sense of usefulness in them. Perhaps the spouse who has fallen ill was the overachiever with a dominant sort of personality, and the illness has allowed the weaker spouse to shine and make a significant contribution to the relationship.

Sadly, the opposite can be true as well. This is not biblical. In marriage, a cord of three strands is necessary: the husband, the wife, and the Holy Spirit. When these three are intertwined, the relationship is strong.

Following the biblical precepts for marriage will keep the marriage strong. Ignoring those precepts will cause the relationship to fray and weaken.

> **Companionship in marriage includes intimacy.**

TWO RELATED CONCEPTS flourish in a biblical marriage that cannot be equally replicated by companionship with a friend: intimacy and vulnerability.

Adam and Eve were naked, and they knew no shame. After the fall, nakedness always implies shame. When Jesus died on the cross, he died naked. The pictures portray him wearing a loincloth, but that is for our sense of modesty. Jesus never sinned, so he had nothing of which to be ashamed, but Jesus took on the sins and the shame of the world. Theologically speaking, his nakedness was the most shameful nakedness there has ever been.

The nakedness between Adam and Eve before the fall was pure and shameless. It was perfect intimacy and perfect vulnerability. They could stand naked before each other with no inclination whatsoever to cover themselves. With boldness, they could stand before the gaze of their spouse with nothing to hide. That is true vulnerability, which leads to blissful intimacy.

Today, many husbands will not allow their wives to know the passcodes to unlock their smartphones. Secret online accounts, secret bank accounts, and secret social profiles are some of the ways spouses hide. This lack of vulnerability has made us experts at concealing, but it comes at the cost of intimacy. Sin has consequences.

In a biblical marriage, a husband and wife can stand naked and vulnerable before one another with no clothes, no makeup, and no secrets. This nakedness allows your spouse to know you more fully than any other person in the world, and that leads to intimacy. Intimacy is fuel for the relationship and fuel for life.

Intimacy is the warmth of life and fellowship. Isolation that comes from concealment is the coldness of death. If you are keeping secrets from your spouse, then you do not have a biblical marriage. You need to be completely open, honest, and vulnerable before your spouse. You may be terrified of telling them your secrets. You may fear rejection, retaliation, and possibly divorce. We wish we could tell you that your fears are invalid. Truthfully, if you have not modeled yourself after the biblical standard, then it is reasonable to expect that your spouse may not respond biblically to your confession and repentance. Be thoughtful and prayerful as you consider your approach. You might need your pastor's help to navigate these difficult waters.

There is an important caveat to this rule of sharing: when confessing sin, be brief. If you cheated on your spouse and you labor over every lurid detail, that is not loving intimacy. You are angry with your spouse and trying to inflict emotional damage. A confession should not glorify sin. Focus the conversation on repairing the relationship.

You will be tempted to accept that you will never be able to live up to this biblical standard, but do not throw in the towel so easily. God equips you to become what he calls you to be, and God made husbands and wives to have honest and intimate relationships.

If you are not experiencing that kind of intimacy, then you are missing out on God's biblical design for your marriage.

> **God is the Architect of your life, and the intimacy that he has designed for you is greater than any substitute you may choose.**

Questions to Consider

- What are some obstacles to intimacy in marriage?
- How might you overcome these obstacles as a couple?

CHAPTER 2:
Leaving and Cleaving

> For this reason, a man will leave his father and mother and be united to his wife, and they will become one flesh.
> **—Genesis 2:24 (NIV)**

> When I was a child, I talked like a child, I thought like a child, I reasoned like a child. When I became a man, I put childish ways behind me.
> **—1 Corinthians 13:11 (NIV)**

It is no secret that our current culture is trending toward perpetual boyhood. In our culture there are boys who refuse to grow up and instead become men who are lazy, irresponsible, cowardly, juvenile, uneducated, and unskilled. Many of these attributes are being touted as virtues by the evolving postmodern community. However, according to God's design, men need to be strong, hardworking, courageous leaders. We must preach the virtue of such manly attributes.

Marriage is for men, not boys!

EVERYBODY LOVES RAYMOND is a famous CBS sitcom that ran from 1996 to 2005. It was quite an entertaining show, but the main character, Raymond, epitomizes the lack of desire to grow up and accept the God-given responsibilities placed upon a man. Ray is a comedian, and as such, he does his job well. However, as a role model, he fails miserably to demonstrate what a biblical husband and father should be. His chief failing is expressed in his desire to be his mommy's little boy. He does not embrace the biblical concept of leaving and cleaving, and while the show gets some laughs at how that sin creates havoc in his marriage, it will not be as funny when your marriage starts to crumble. Pain is funny, but from a distance. We do not want your marriage to be fodder for a comedy show; so grow up and learn to shoulder responsibility.

> Children, obey your parents in everything, for this pleases the Lord.
> **—Colossians 3:20 (NIV)**

> Honor your father and your mother, so that you may live long in the land the LORD your God is giving you.
> **—Exodus 20:12 (NIV)**

Children are commanded to obey; adults are commanded to honor. There is a distinction. After the leaving, we are still expected to honor our parents, but the dynamics of the relationship have changed dramatically. If you are married but still live like a child, then you do not have a biblical marriage.

> **Manhood requires adopting responsibility.**

DRINKING BEER, GROWING facial hair, and spitting tobacco are not manhood. Manhood requires adopting responsibility. If you are living with your parents, playing video games, and waiting for your mother to bring you a snack after she finishes folding your laundry, you are not a man yet. You are not ready for a biblical marriage. You need to leave childhood behind before you are capable of cleaving to the wife with whom God blesses you.

> So be strong, show yourself a man...
> **—1 Kings 2:2 (NIV)**

What does being a man look like? For starters, you need to get a job. Find a place to live where your authority can take root. Pay your bills with money you have earned. Do your laundry. Cook your meals. Wash your dishes. Clean your house. Make your doctor and dentist appointments. Take care of the maintenance on your truck. Learn to do these things for yourself before you take a wife so that you will be strong. You need to be strong enough to do these for yourself and have enough strength left over to take care of the wife and children with whom God blesses you. If you look for a wife who can take the place of your mother so you can continue to live like a child, then you will not have a biblical marriage. You will not be a man, just a comedian, not a leader or someone to be admired but someone to be mocked, the butt of a joke.

I know I have spent time coaching up the men, mainly because this command is specifically given to the man, but this is a two-sided street. Leaving and cleaving also involves the wife coming under the subjection of her new husband. In a wedding ceremony, there is often a moment when the father of the bride will hand the bride's hand over to the groom. This is symbolic, but it is also very meaningful. In marriage, the wife is leaving one home permanently to become a part of another. Leaving and cleaving to your husband means leaving your father and mother.

Too many couples fail to leave, and as a result, they fail to cleave. This is not to say that you must cut all ties to your parents once you marry. This is to say that the most important person for you to spend time with, speak with, and serve is your spouse. It can be very frustrating for a husband or wife to marry and then have to compete with their spouse's parents for attention and devotion. So we encourage you with the biblical command: leave and cleave to each other.

Questions to Consider

- In what ways do you specifically need to grow in order to be ready to obey the command to "leave and cleave"?
- What might be some major obstacles to your ability to leave and cleave?

CHAPTER 3:
Covenant, Not Contract

It is important that we not view marriage as a contract but rather as a covenant. The covenant concept offers the appropriate mindset. The appropriate mindset will affect your thoughts, actions, and reactions.

The Old Testament (OT) does not speak of "making" a covenant but rather of "cutting" a covenant. When two people cut a covenant, they would cut animals in half, and the two covenant cutters would walk between the halves, saying something to the effect of, "May I become like these butchered animals if I do not fulfill my part of the covenant." The covenant between God and Abraham involved the cutting of animals and then later the cutting of the foreskin, which typifies the OT mental concept that covenants are cut. ***A covenant that is cut is serious and sacred.***

Our current culture thinks in terms of contracts. The contract relationship states that the first party will carry out his part of the agreement in consideration for the other party carrying out her part of the agreement. If he does not keep up his end of the contract, then she is not obligated to keep up her end. Contracts are useful business tools, but if your mental picture of marriage resembles a contract, then you do not have a biblical marriage.

Marriage is a covenant. That means that even if your spouse does not act like the husband (or wife) who is described in God's Word, you are still obligated to act like the spouse who is described in God's Word.

The divorce rate has dipped slightly, but that is because many couples are skipping the marriage vows in favor of cohabitating.[4] The data regarding marriage and divorce is not biblically accurate because the data follows government guidelines regarding the definition of marriage instead of the Bible.

If we endeavor to be as biblical as possible, what is the essence of marriage? "And they will become one flesh," (Gen. 2:24 NIV). That is the original statement that defined the original marriage.

Strictly speaking, when a man and a woman become one flesh (have sex), they have entered into marriage. Their bodies have made a covenant, even if their lawyers have not.

If the data regarding marriage and divorce followed the biblical definition, then the divorce rate would be much higher. Skewing the data to ignore men and women who cohabitate as husband and wife without the legal document causes the divorce rate to be lowered artificially and does not gauge how well society is conforming to biblical values. *In other words, relationships between husbands and wives are worse than the statistics indicate.*

4 Aaron Earls (@WardrobeDoor) lifewayresearch.com/2018/09/26/millennials-are-lowering-the-divorce-rate-but-not-everyone-is-benefiting/.

"Free Love" Rejects the Covenant

Before the invention of the birth control pill, "free love" was devastating for women for obvious reasons. Men driven by carnal desires would steal the youth of women, get them pregnant, and then move on to new conquests. Such men had to be shamed by society into taking responsibility for a family that they had created.

Since the pill came onto the market, the number of women participating in "free love" has risen. It is an erroneous conclusion to believe that just because the pill keeps you from starting a family, engaging in "free love" is free of consequences. Nevertheless, many women have followed the unbiblical example that ungodly men have modeled for so long. Sin has painful consequences.

This behavior from women has created an interesting and sad phenomenon among men called "men going their own way" (MGTOW). So many men have been hurt by women who easily leave a relationship to trade up that these injured men have banded together via the internet to discourage each other from ever having a committed relationship with women. They do not believe in being yoked together at all. They take themselves off the market. MGTOW is the male version of a feminist who says a woman does not need a man.

Feminists are at one end of the spectrum, and MGTOW are at the other end, preaching the same message to the different genders. They are both wrong.

The truth is that both men and women are hard to live with, and that is why a covenant is so important. We don't get to walk away until death do us part. We stay in the fight and find a way to make the relationship work.

> **There is no such thing as free love. Loving someone is the most expensive thing you will ever do.**

One Flesh Is a Covenant

God pronounced the first wedding vows (covenant) in the Garden of Eden when he said, "For this reason a man will leave his father and mother [cut ties] and be united to his wife, and they will become one flesh" (Gen. 2:24, NIV). The union implies a covenant, not a contract. The two becoming one flesh implies cutting. When a man becomes one with his wife, he penetrates her and pierces (cuts) the hymen, causing a flow of blood. Marriage is a covenant of blood. Jesus adds unto these words from Genesis with "Therefore what God has joined together, let man not separate" (Mark 10:9 NIV).

> It [wisdom] will save you also from the adulteress, from the wayward wife with her seductive words, who has left the partner of her youth and ignored the <u>covenant</u> she made before God.
> **—Proverbs 2:16–17 (NIV emphasis mine)**

Hosea Exemplifies the Covenant

The relationship between the prophet Hosea and his wife, Gomer, provides an excellent illustration of covenant love (Hosea 1–3). In chapter 1, Hosea is commanded by God to take a wife of adultery, and the prophet obeys by marrying Gomer. They have three children together.

In chapter 2, through poetic language, we learn that Gomer has returned to her old ways. Presumably, she did not find the compensation of being a preacher's wife to be sufficient to keep her in the lifestyle to which she had become accustomed. She went out to make money the old-fashioned way, and in doing so, she disgraced and humiliated her husband.

As we all know, being young and beautiful is a temporary state. Some people are adept at making beauty last longer than others, but all forms of physical beauty fade. Gomer's beauty faded to the extent that her work dwindled, and she could not pay the bills; she was eventually sold as a slave on the auction block. We may presume that she was humiliated with nakedness (Hosea 2:10) on the auction block. That was typical so the bidders could see what they might purchase.

When she was standing there on the auction block, she had nothing to offer Hosea. She had not come close to fulfilling her part of the contract. But marriage is not a contract. It is a covenant. So Hosea went to the auction and purchased (redeemed) his wife (Hosea 3).

This is when Hosea's love comes the closest to the perfect love of God. If you had the perfect wife, how difficult would it be to love her? How extraordinary would your love be if your wife were extraordinary in every aspect? The excellent qualities of your wife attract you toward her, but covenant love and attraction are not the same. Attraction will ebb and flood like the tide. Covenant love persists.

Extraordinary love is covenant love. Physical attraction does not sustain a marriage, but the covenant of marriage sustains the love. Covenant love persists when the object of love seems utterly unlovable.

The more lovable the object of your love, the more gratification you may receive as she reciprocates and returns your affection. When her most attractive qualities wane, the importance of your covenant love for her rises to the surface. Marital love comes closest to the perfect love of God when a spouse who appears unworthy of affection is loved. That is covenant love.

Marriage is a type.[5] It is a symbol that God has embedded into his creation to portray the covenant love of God for his people. The church is the bride, and Jesus Christ is the groom (Rev. 19:7, 21:2). Our marriages should represent the marriage between Christ and the church. Our marriages are a type, and the marriage between Christ and the church is the archetype.

5 In this instance, *type* means a person or thing symbolizing or exemplifying the ideal. The ideal would be the archetype.

> **Covenant love is unconditional love.**

But God demonstrates his own love for us in this:
While we were still sinners, Christ died for us.
—Romans 5:8 (NIV)

WHEN WE TRANSGRESS against this type, we lie about the nature of God. When we treat marriages as contracts, we betray the archetype and slander the character of God's love for his people.

One fall during a presidential election, I became quite disgusted with the belligerent and hostile personalities emanating from the TV set. I turned to a channel that is well known for its positive and romantic movies. In the first movie, a man and woman had been dating but realized they were not meant for each other. They said something to the effect of, "If we have to work this hard at it, it must not be love; we must not be soulmates." Then they had the most amicable breakup I have ever seen. The lady went on to meet her "soulmate." She fell deeply in love and enjoyed an intimate relationship that seemed effortless. Then I watched another movie. It was the same plot with different actors. By the third movie, my soul had been purged of the obnoxious political diatribe, and I began to think critically about romance movies.

The movies all seemed to be based on the presupposition that love does not require work or effort. They suggest that if it is not effortless, then it is not love. They suggest that if your partner irritates you or fails to satisfy you in every way, then you have not found your soulmate. They imply that you should quit the relationship and keep looking.

They are wrong! This idea that a person quits when the going gets tough is a major contributing factor to the high divorce rate. *Love is not found in the absence of work. The work testifies to the love*.

No one is perfect, and that demands work from both husband and wife. In the history of the world, there has never been a perfect bride. *The Lord Jesus Christ is the only perfect groom, and he did excruciating work on the cross to make his bride beautiful so that the relationship would work*. If your marriage is going to be biblical and successful, it is not because you have found your "soulmate." It is because you are willing to put in the necessary work.

Baptist preachers are not known for making great toasts, but I think one of the bests toasts that could be made at a wedding would be, "To a marriage that works."

Questions to Consider

- What is the difference between a covenant and a contract?
- Why is it important for you as a couple to understand marriage as a covenant?

CHAPTER 4:
Equally Yoked

The Bible has two absolutes when it comes to whom you may and may not marry. First, you must marry someone of the opposite sex. Second, you must marry someone of the same faith. Paul discusses this in 2 Corinthians.

> Do not be unequally yoked together with unbelievers. For what fellowship has righteousness with lawlessness? And what communion has light with darkness? Or what harmony has Christ with Belial, or what has a believer in common with an unbeliever?
> **—2 Corinthians 6:14–15 (NKJV)**

Paul uses the metaphor of being "yoked" together with an unbeliever. Most of us have not plowed behind a yoke of oxen so the meaning of the metaphor might elude us, but we can grasp his point: if you have a big strong ox yoked together with a little, short, weak ox (or yoked to a small mule), then you will have trouble plowing in a straight line. The bigger animal is going to outstep the weaker animal, causing you to plow in circles. By the same token, if you are a Christian and struggling to follow Jesus, and then you marry a non-Christian who makes no effort to follow Jesus, your marriage is going to go in circles.

Again, the marriage between husband and wife is correlated to the marriage between Christ and the church. Your marriage is a type; the relationship between Christ and the church is the archetype. If a Christian marries a non-Christian, he is going against the archetype, the biblical picture of marriage. He is signifying and symbolizing a union between Christ and Belial (Satan). Such a statement is false and blasphemous. It is sinful, and sin has consequences.

The Bible does make an allowance for unbelievers who are married but one of them gets saved. If the unbeliever is willing to live with you in your new Christian faith, then do not divorce the unbeliever (1 Cor. 7:12–17). This is not ideal, but it makes the best of a difficult situation. However, when it comes to entering into a marriage, the believer is to obey this command and not unite with the unbeliever. ***To the young woman who is considering a marriage proposal, her most pertinent question is, "If I marry him, will he lead me closer to Jesus?"*** If he is not a Christian believer, then he will not lead you closer to Jesus, and you should not marry him.

If we think carefully about this at all, we will quickly realize the wisdom behind this command. ***Since God desires that we grow in our faith and become more like Jesus Christ as we become more mature in our faith, then it just makes sense that the person with whom we share our most***

intimate earthly relationship (our spouse), should be on that same journey of sanctification. They are then sharing in the same journey, as they both seek to follow Christ more closely in their life.

This is the believer's fundamental purpose—to become more like Jesus and follow him with his or her life. It doesn't make sense that the believer's closest friend and the most intimate sharer of life would be someone who disagrees with them on the fundamental purpose of life. If our life's purpose is at odds with our spouse, then so, too, will be our practices.

Indeed, many practical struggles will inevitably prove difficult for the believer who unites with an unbeliever:

- The unbeliever will not understand the need to be intimately involved in the church.
- The unbeliever will grow frustrated that the believer takes a whole day and sets it aside for the Lord and his worship.
- The unbeliever will not understand nor agree with the believer's need to give sacrificially to the work of the Lord.
- There will be disagreements on what is best for their children, not only concerning church but also with other aspects of life.
- The unbeliever will hinder the believer's ability to fulfill the Great Commission.

Parable of Bill and Jill

Imagine with me for a moment—Bill and Jill go to the same college. They have both been out on dates with several people, but nothing has turned serious.

One day, Bill walks into the local coffee shop and orders one medium caramel frappé with chocolate chips added. Then Bill steps aside and waits for his drink. A few minutes later, a beautiful young lady named Jill walks into the same coffee shop. Jill approaches the register and orders one medium caramel frappé with chocolate chips added. Upon finishing her order, she steps aside to wait. Almost immediately, the barista loudly shouts, "One caramel frappé with chocolate chips!" Upon hearing this, both Bill and Jill step forward to claim the drink. They look at each other, and Jill asks Bill, "Did you order that same drink?" And Bill says, "I sure did, but you can have that one, and I'll wait on the one you ordered."

They both laugh at the fact that they ordered the same thing. They strike up a conversation. They end up sharing a table at the coffee shop to drink their identical drinks. One thing leads to another, and Bill asks Jill to go out on a date.

The two begin dating and talking with each other all the time. Bill likes Jill. She's pretty. She's sweet. She's on time when he comes to pick her up. She's not extravagant and is fine with going out on cheap dates. She loves football and going to games. For Bill, these are the most important things to find in a girl.

Jill likes Bill too. He's handsome. He's a gentleman. He shows up on time to pick her up. They have so much in common. They even ordered the same weird drink at the coffee shop.

But there's one thing that has troubled Jill. One Saturday night, she asked Bill to go to church with her the following Sunday, but he told her that he did not do that sort of thing. She asked him what he believed about God, and Bill explained to her that he didn't believe in anything. He just felt like he was supposed to be a good person and live his life the best he knew how.

This troubled Jill because Jill is a committed follower of Jesus Christ. She loves to serve the church and participate in the ministry of the church.

For a while, Jill compromises on her belief that she should be dating a believer, but before long, it's clear that Bill has different priorities. He will not go to church with her. He consistently gets frustrated at her desire to take up her entire Sunday with church activities. She thought she could change him, but it is clear that he is bent on doing what he desires. Though it is painful, Jill does the right thing and ends the relationship with Bill. It turns out that you need more in common than just the drink you order at the coffee shop.

Again, if the two are not in agreement on the primary purpose of life, then how can they possibly agree on the secondary issues that arise? They can't. They won't.

The common refrain when most Christians hear these strong words is the belief that they can change the person they are marrying, as if God has made an exception for them and is sending them into an evangelistic marriage in which they have been given the task of changing the heart of their spouse. That sounds holy, but there is a problem with this mindset. We as individuals cannot change anyone. As a pastor, I have no personal ability to change the hearts and lives of the people who walk into my church on a Sunday morning. All I can do is point them to the One who can change their life, but I do not possess the power to regenerate their dead heart and bring them to faith in Christ. And neither do you. God is the one who changes hearts and lives, not us.

So to think that you can change someone is presumptive. You are claiming to be able to do something that you cannot do. Now this is not to say that sometimes believers have disobeyed this command and entered into relationships with unbelievers, and then God saved the unbelievers. I'm sure that has been the case many times, and I praise God for that. However, that still is disobedience to this command, and that outcome is by no means a guarantee that it will always work out that way.

That is not typically the way it goes. More often, the believer tends to follow the lifestyle of the unbeliever and is consequently dragged into a life of sin and rebellion.

This is why it is incredibly important for a believer to be united with another believer in marriage. This ensures that both are working and striving for the same goal. They are both working to be obedient to God. They are both striving to live their lives with the glory of God in mind. This collective purpose will unite the two like nothing else. They will be unified on Sundays when it is time to get ready for church. They will be unified when it comes to obeying God's command to give to the purposes of the Lord. They will be unified when it comes to raising their children in the Word of the Lord.

Finally, concerning this principle, I believe that the key to a God-honoring marriage is repentance and forgiveness. A husband and wife will inevitably fail each other. I fail my wife all the time, and I cannot imagine what it would be like living with someone who did not know or understand the depth of grace and forgiveness that we have received by the cross of Jesus Christ.

The forgiveness we both have received from Jesus forms the foundation for our ability to forgive one another. In Ephesians 4:32 (NAS), Paul gave this command that applies to all believers:

> Be kind to one another, tender-hearted, forgiving each other, just as God in Christ also has forgiven you.

The basis and example of our forgiveness is the fact that we both have been forgiven. As Christian husbands and wives, we operate with the understanding that we are both sinners. We both desperately need the Gospel of Jesus Christ and the forgiveness that is given through Jesus.

How can a believer expect an unbeliever to understand grace and forgiveness if they have not yet entered into a relationship with Jesus Christ? Forgiveness and repentance are vital when it comes to living in union and harmony with another sinner.

This is truly the beauty of Christian marriage. A Christian marriage is like all marriages because the marriage bond brings together two sinners. A Christian marriage is unlike all marriages because the Christian marriage bond brings together two sinners who have been forgiven and thus have a foundation for extending forgiveness to each other.

Questions to Consider

- **Have you discussed your beliefs about God with your prospective spouse?**
- **What differences do you have?**
- **Are you equally yoked?**

CHAPTER 5:
Leadership and Love

I have always enjoyed competition, from the days of childhood until now. Specifically, I have always enjoyed any game or sport that involved a ball. I grew up playing baseball and football in the front yard with my two brothers and basketball in the church parking lot next door. Having two older brothers, one five years older, and the other seven years older, I was always at a disadvantage when trying to compete. Nevertheless, I honed my skills in baseball and basketball so that when high school tryouts for baseball and basketball came, I was excited to try out and play for both teams.

One difficulty I found in getting older was the abrupt stoppage of involvement in team sports. Unless you are talented enough to go play at the collegiate level or the pro level, most people's sports careers end upon high school graduation. Such was the case with me. However, because I still enjoyed competition, I picked up a new sport in my twenties: golf.

Golf is a different and frustrating game in many ways because it is uniquely individualistic. All the good and all the bad come from your performance. If you slice your drive off the tee into the woods, you are the sole responsible party for the poor shot. If it takes you five strokes to get your ball out of a sand bunker, those five strokes will be added to your score. If you miss a putt, it is your fault. Unlike in other sports, you cannot hide behind or blame a teammate or even your competitor for poor performance in golf. The responsibility for your performance lies solely on you.

Marriage is not like golf. ***Marriage is comparable to a team sport and takes the cooperative, sacrificial effort of both individuals involved for the team to succeed.*** What this means for marriage specifically is that both the husband and the wife must sacrifice themselves for the other for the benefit of their marriage.

Many of the problems we see today in marriage are due to the lack of understanding about this principle. Too many couples are fractured by individualistic mindsets. This is demonstrated by husbands and wives who care much about their own desires and little about the desires of the other. The willingness for separation and divorce flows from the idea of one individual concluding that he or she would be better off without the other. The point of marriage is not about being better off without your spouse; instead, biblical marriage is about both parties being better off *because* both are sacrificially giving themselves to the other in submission to God's design in marriage.

When we consider the commands in Scripture for both husbands and wives, it is clear that God desires marriage to be an exercise of sacrificial love by both the husband and the wife. The Apostle Paul, in his letter to the church of Ephesus, made this principle abundantly clear.

To wives, he wrote:

> Wives, *be subject* to your own husbands, *as to the Lord.* For the husband is the head of the wife, as Christ also is the head of the church, He Himself being the Savior of the body. But *as the church is subject to Christ, so also the wives ought to be to their husbands in everything.*
> **(Eph. 5:22–24 NAS; emphasis added)**

A wife who desires to follow God's command in Scripture will sacrificially submit herself to the godly leadership of her husband. Submission, by definition, involves the entrustment of leadership to another. The wife biblically loves her husband by submitting to his leadership and headship within the home. She does this for the benefit of her husband, and this is her sacrificial contribution to the marriage.

To husbands, he wrote:

> Husbands, love your wives, just as Christ also loved the church and *gave Himself up for her*, that *He might sanctify her, having cleansed her by the washing of water with the word, that He might present to Himself the church in all her glory, having no spot or wrinkle or any such*

thing; but that she would be holy and blameless. So husbands ought also to love their own wives as their own bodies. *He who loves his own wife loves himself; for no one ever hated his own flesh, but nourishes and cherishes it, just as Christ also does the church,* because we are members of His body.

(Eph. 5:25–30 NAS; emphasis added)

Husbands have a unique responsibility in the home. The husband is to lead the home and be a consistent picture of Jesus Christ, who sacrificially gave himself up for the benefit of his bride (the church). So husbands, too, are to give themselves up for the benefit of their wives. Practically speaking, the husband is to be the most selfless person in the home, willing to sacrifice himself for the benefit of all those under his leadership. This is often not the case, and this is at least one reason why marriages are struggling in our current culture.

At the root of this problem is the misconception of what it means to be a man and the leader of the home. Make no mistake: Paul writes to the church of Ephesus that the husband is to be the head of the wife. In other words, he is to be the leader of the home. From the very beginning, when Adam and Eve were in the Garden of Eden, we see clearly that the home suffers whenever the husband fails in this regard. If he doesn't lead, then he has failed in his responsibility as the head.

Some have noted personality differences in the marriage—for example, when the wife is stronger willed, and the husband is more passive; thus, it just makes sense for the wife to be the leader in that situation. However, personality is not the authority or ruler over our hearts. If we are Christians, then Jesus Christ is Lord, and his design for marriage is the ruling authority over our lives. Consequently, then, it is harmful, not harmless, to allow the roles to reverse in the marriage. To state it even more plainly, for the husband to relinquish the leadership of the home to the wife is a sin. It is going defiantly against God's design for marriage, and it will not end well. The husband is the head of the wife.

This brings us back to the point of sacrifice. Paul makes it clear that the husband is the head of the wife, and then he follows up that statement with how that headship is meant to play out. It is meant to be played out through the husband's love and sacrificial life. Headship in the home does not mean the husband is to selfishly sit back like a king while all his subjects cater to his every whim and desire. That is more reflective of a worldly man. The godly husband sacrifices his energy, his effort, his time, and his life for the benefit of his wife and the benefit of the collective family.

Marriages struggle because one or both individuals fail to heed the clear directives of Scripture, as outlined in Ephesians 5. A wife who fails to submit to her husband as God has designed will strain the marriage, and if she continues in prolonged disobedience, it will be practically impossible for the marriage relationship to thrive. So, too, a selfish husband who thinks only about his benefit will strain the marriage, and prolonged disobedience to this clear command will inevitably result in the failure of the marriage.

Parable of Bill and Jill

Bill works a blue-collar job five days a week. He works outside in the heat and cold, depending on the season. His hands are rough and greasy, and his clothes always reek when he gets home. Every weekday, Bill gets up at 5:00 a.m., drinks half a pot of black coffee, and goes to work. He returns home at 6:00 p.m.

Jill is a teacher at the local elementary school. She wakes up every weekday, fixes her lunch, and heads off to school, where she deals with first graders all day long. She wipes noses, dries tears, and has almost no adult interaction throughout the day. She makes it home around 4:00 p.m.

When Bill arrives home, his only desire is to take a shower, sit in his recliner, watch TV, and rest until it's time to go to bed. When Jill arrives home, her only desire is to have some adult interaction with her husband, Bill.

But Bill's desire to rest and watch TV is in direct opposition to Jill's desire for interaction.

What will they do?

Bill is not wrong to desire rest at the end of a hard day. Jill is not wrong to desire adult interaction after spending all day with first graders. So what must happen for the marriage to thrive is sacrifice. Bill must lead by sacrificing some time to interact with his wife because he understands that is her greatest desire. Jill must submit to Bill's need for rest and give him some time to do that. Both can happen, but both must sacrifice for the good of the other.

The key to a successful marriage is submitting to the design of the One who originally designed it.

The beauty of a marriage that does submit to God's design is a marriage that beautifully paints a picture of the Gospel of Jesus Christ. This is why Paul says of marriage in Ephesians 5:32: "This mystery is great; but I am speaking with reference to Christ and the church." Marriage, as God intended it, is to be the clearest earthly picture of the Gospel to the watching world. Sadly, many marriages have marred this beautiful picture by seeking to go individual ways by living in rebellion to God's design.

Sacrificial love is not easy. Sacrificial love is supremely difficult because it means that you must put away the natural tendency to pursue your benefit and instead pursue the benefit of your spouse. There will be times in marriage when obeying this principle will be more difficult than others. However, this is God's design, and this is the way the marriage team succeeds. When we submit to his good design, both are better off because both are giving themselves up for the other.

Questions to Consider

- Prospective groom: What is your role inside the home?
- Prospective bride: What is your role inside the home?

CHAPTER 6:
Sex Matters

Sexual intercourse is a gift from God. It must be employed for the continuation of the species. It is obvious that if everyone on earth became abstinent, then the human race would be one generation away from extinction.

Life is sexually transmitted.

> God blessed them and said to them, "Be fruitful and increase in number; fill the earth and subdue it. Rule over the fish of the sea and the birds of the air and over every living creature that moves on the ground."
> **—Genesis 1:28 (NIV)**

> Then God blessed Noah and his sons, saying to them, "Be fruitful and increase in number and fill the earth."
> **—Genesis 9:1 (NIV)**

> Your wife will be like a fruitful vine within your house; your sons will be like olive shoots around your table.
> **—Psalm 128:3 (NIV)**

> Daughters of Jerusalem, I charge you by the gazelles and by the does of the field: Do not arouse or awaken love until it so desires.
> **—Song of Solomon 2:7 (NIV)**

ABSTINENCE IS THE RULE BEFORE MARRIAGE. *Abstinence includes foreplay.* In the Song of Solomon, the two main characters are becoming husband and wife. The woman teaches the young ladies that they should not engage in foreplay before the appointed time. The "ladies in waiting" are not on the precipice of marriage and therefore should not arouse or awaken love.

If you are going to light a fire tomorrow, don't strike the match today. Single people should not only abstain from sexual relations but also the foreplay that leads to sex. How long can you play with matches before something catches fire?

After marriage, have a robust sex life!

Many long-winded Christians have preached hard against sexual activity. Many young Christians have been raised on a steady diet of *"Don't have sex!"* But when a young Christian gets married, the refrain needs to be reversed: *"Have sex with your spouse!"*

You slander God when you slander a healthy and robust sexual relationship within the bounds of marriage. Sexual intercourse must be employed for the continuation of the species, but more than that, it must be enjoyed if you are going to have a biblical marriage.

When I conduct premarital counseling for young couples, they often have to refrain from snickering when I bring up the subject of sex. They do not wish to be disrespectful to their pastor, but they are thinking, "There may be many things we have to work on to have a biblical marriage, but sex is not going to be a problem." The top two reasons for divorce are sexual problems (usually adultery) and stress created by financial debt. If sexual intercourse between a husband and wife is so easy, then why is the divorce rate so high? You need to work diligently to make sure you have a healthy and robust sex life with your spouse.

Marriage Means Consent

In February of 2000, Fox aired a show, *Who Wants to Marry a Millionaire?* A real-life multimillionaire got to choose his bride from fifty contestants, women who volunteered to be on the show. After the multimillionaire chose his bride, they were married on air. The chosen woman later said she went on the show as a lark and could not believe the stranger kissed her on the lips after they had taken their marital vows. Usually, people who make wedding vows expect to be kissed, and more. To put it mildly, that TV marriage was not a biblical marriage. I can understand how the woman did not equate that circus act with an actual marriage. The

marriage was never consummated, and the annulment was finalized in April 2000.

In a biblical marriage, you consent to a sexual relationship, and if you withhold sex for a selfish reason, such as hurting or manipulating your spouse, then you do not have a biblical marriage.

> The husband should fulfill his marital duty to his wife, and likewise the wife to her husband. The wife's body does not belong to her alone but also to her husband. In the same way, the husband's body does not belong to him alone but also to his wife. Do not deprive each other except by mutual consent and for a time, so that you may devote yourselves to prayer. Then come together again so that Satan will not tempt you because of your lack of self-control.
> **—1 Corinthians 7:3–5 (NIV)**

> I am my lover's and my lover is mine.
> **—Song of Solomon 6:3 (NIV)**

This particular admonition to have sexual intercourse may be more difficult for the bride than the groom for a variety of reasons. Biology, physiology, and psychology are significant factors that can make it difficult for young brides to enjoy sex as much as the grooms.

The difference between testosterone and estrogen is one such biological factor. Testosterone responds differently than estrogen to many different types of exercise.

Regarding sexual appetite, testosterone drives the groom much more powerfully than the bride, who is driven by estrogen. A healthy young groom who has relations with his bride three times a week will consider such frequency to be meager. A healthy young bride will consider once every two weeks to be adequate. Such are the differences between testosterone and estrogen.

A major physiological difference would be the amount of pain a woman might endure during sex. If she is not aroused, then penetration is going to be painful and unpleasant. Such an experience will cross over to become a psychological problem. She will equate sex with pain inflicted upon her by her husband.

The typical sexual encounter is thought to have four stages: (1) desire, (2) arousal, (3) climax, and (4) the refractory period. It may be useful to know that research indicates that for many people, arousal comes before desire. In other words, if you wait until you feel like it to have sex, then you are never going to have sex, but if you start the foreplay and physical arousal, the desire (appetite for sex) will follow.

Maureen McGrath, author of *Sex & Health*, jokes that if you never want to have sex again, get married. She says that on average, young people start having sex ten years before marriage, and the frequency of sex declines after marriage.[6] Her data may be correct, but it does not represent the biblical ideal, and while she does not speak from a biblical perspective, she goes on to describe the sadness that comes from these nonbiblical lifestyles. Sin has consequences.

According to a recent survey, the number of sexless marriages in Japan is shocking. Reportedly, 47.2 percent of marriages between men and women are sexless.[7] The highest rate was among those in their forties. Among married men, over 35 percent said they worked so many hours that they were too tired for intercourse.

The birth rate in Japan is declining, and the population is expected to drop from 127 million to 86 million in the next forty years. In addition to internet pornography, which is available around the world, Japan is heavily invested in sex robots. One Japanese man married his sex robot.[8] Apparently, a sexual relationship with your spouse is too much effort. Why put in the work when there is an effortless, robotic relationship available?

6   Maureen McGrath, "No Sex Marriage—Masturbation, Loneliness, Cheating and Shame," TEDxStanleyPark July 6, 2016, 21:52, http://youtu.be/LVgzOyHVcj4.

7   Justin McCurry, "Record Numbers of Couples Living in Sexless Marriages in Japan, Says Report," February 14, 2017, The Guardian, https://amp.theguardian.com/world/2017/feb/14/record-numbers-of-couples-living-in-sexless-marriages-in-japan-says-report.

8   Alex Williams, "Today We Fall in Love through Our Phones. Maybe Your Phone Itself Could Be Just as Satisfying?," January 19, 2019, The New York Times, https://www.nytimes.com/2019/01/19/style/sex-robots.amp.html.

If you are going to have a biblical marriage, you need to make the effort and work through the problems. It will require you to have some difficult discussions. Intimacy, honesty, and vulnerability play crucial roles in these discussions. The sooner you have these discussions, the better off you will be. If these problems fester, bitterness will set in, which usually leads to other unbiblical behavior, such as pornography and adultery. You may even find yourselves on the path to separation. Even if you can tough it out, why wait ten years to tell your spouse what you like in bed? If you ignore your spouse's needs in the bedroom, then you do not have a biblical marriage.

Questions to Consider

- **What is the purpose of sex inside of a marriage?**
- **How can you glorify God through sex in your marriage?**

CHAPTER 7:
Pornography

Put to death, therefore, whatever belongs to your earthly nature: sexual immorality, impurity, lust, evil desires and greed, which is idolatry. Because of these, the wrath of God is coming.
—Colossians 3:5–6 (NIV)

Pornography leads to death—the deaths of individuals, deaths of marriages, deaths of families. You cannot have a biblical marriage if pornography is part of your life. God's Word says to put to death sexual immorality. Pornography is sexually immoral. It has no place in a Christian's life or within a biblical marriage.

Paul commands the church of Colossae in the passage above to put to death those things that invoke the wrath of God. God's wrath is coming against all sin, so it is the Christian's duty to put to death those things that are against the heart and nature of God. Christians ought to be actively killing areas of sin in their lives.

Pornography is included in those things that a Christian ought to put to death. ***Pornography is rooted in fleshly lust and is adultery of the heart and the mind.*** Oftentimes, people may look at pornography as less of a sin because there is no physical interaction with the other person, but we find in Holy Scripture that the lust involved in viewing pornography is indeed adultery. In the eyes of God, to look at someone who is not your spouse in a lustful manner is adultery.

Pornography is a big deal. It is sin against your spouse, your body, and ultimately against God. It is a sin that expresses rebellion against the Holy God who created you.

William Struthers expresses the importance of understanding purity as a matter of both the mind and the body. He writes,

> Purity is as much a matter of the mind as it is of the body, and it is important not to separate the two. The thoughts we think affect our body. The behaviors that we engage in affect our thinking... Thoughts and behavior are woven together and intertwined with one another. This is how pornography and unhealthy sexuality pollutes the brain and the body together.[9]

Jesus made it clear in Matthew 5 in the Sermon on the Mount that lustfully looking is adultery. He said this:

You have heard that it was said, "You shall not commit adultery." But I tell you that anyone who looks at a woman lustfully has already committed adultery with her in his

---

9 William Struthers, *Wired for Intimacy: How Pornography Hijacks the Male Brain* (Downers Grove, IL: Intervarsity Press, 2009), 28.

heart. If your right eye causes you to stumble, gouge it out and throw it away. It is better for you to lose one part of your body than for your whole body to be thrown into hell. And if your right hand causes you to stumble, cut it off and throw it away. It is better for you to lose one part of your body than for your whole body to go into hell. (Matt. 5:27–30 NIV)

Jesus speaks to the common belief of the world that minimizes the act of lust. Jesus takes the commandment even further to the thoughts and intentions of the heart. So then, we must not be so naive to adopt the worldly mantra "You can look, but you cannot touch." Jesus said in **Matthew 6:22–23 (NAS): "The eye is the lamp of the body; if therefore your eye is clear, your whole body will be full of light. But if your eye is bad, your whole body will be full of darkness. If therefore the light that is in you is darkness, how great is the darkness!"**

> Pornography poisons the eye and the mind, and it destroys marriages.

WHEN EXAMINING THE words of Jesus, and then thinking about what occurs when someone looks at pornography, it is very clear what Jesus's understanding of pornography would be. We can conclude that lustfully looking at pornography is adultery. When you look at pornography and lust, you are committing adultery against your spouse and God.

Many passages in the Bible are difficult to understand and interpret, but this is not one of them. Jesus condemned the act of looking lustfully at others who are not your spouse.

There are countless stories in today's world of husbands having been caught in the act of looking at pornography.

Parable of Bill and Jill

Jill recently discovered that her husband Bill was looking at pornography. Imagine Jill's heartbreak at the thought of Bill looking at other women to please himself. What Bill should have been finding in Jill, he found in another woman whom he did not know. The woman he had pledged his life to, had children with, and spent every night with for years is now dealing with the fact that Bill is fantasizing and looking at other women in ways he had never looked at her.

It is easy to understand how Jill would then wonder what Bill was thinking about when they are intimate. ***The irreparable harm done by his sin would permanently be etched in the back of her mind!*** *Much like a spouse who has been the victim of an extramarital affair, Jill would forever question Bill's commitment to her as long as his phone was nearby.*

> **This is adultery in the heart,
> and it has no place in a biblical marriage.**

WE WANT TO encourage you to take action now to prevent this from becoming an issue inside your marriage. If this has been a temptation in the past, then put safety measures in place. Add an internet filter. Have a confidante you trust who will hold you accountable. Be honest and work together to rid your marriage of this sin.

Questions to Consider

- **How may it affect your marriage if this particular sin of pornography were to take root in your life?**
- **What measures will you take right now to guard against this sin in your life?**

CHAPTER 8:
Communication Matters

Husbands and wives need to learn to communicate with one another. This requires effort and a particular type of thinking known as discernment. Study your spouse's communication habits, and discern how to speak to him or her in a way that effectively communicates.

Studies vary as to how many words per day women out-speak men. Some studies say the difference is negligible, and others say it is significant.[10] Many husbands will embody the strong, silent stereotype. One such example would be President Calvin Coolidge, who was known as Silent Cal.

The story is told that the famous wit, Dorothy Parker, was once seated by President Calvin Coolidge at a dinner party. "Miss Parker said to the president that she had bet a friend that during the course of the meal she could make him say more than five words.

"You lose," the president said.

Or so the story goes. There are many such stories about Calvin Coolidge sitting through entire social events without uttering a word. He himself said, "If you don't say anything,

10   See for example, https://www.dailymail.co.uk/sciencetech/article-2281891/Women-really-talk-men-13-000-words-day-precise.html.

you won't be called on to repeat it" and "I have never been hurt by what I have not said." Other sayings include "You can't know too much, but you can say too much" and "No man ever listened himself out of a job."[11]

There are plenty of people who talk too much, but there are people who say too little. We should be quick to listen and slow to speak (James 1:19), but perpetual silence is an abdication of responsibility. Leaders are expected to verbalize a vision, for "where there is no vision, the people perish," (Prov. 29:17, KJV). Leaders need to verbalize direction and encouragement toward the fulfillment of that vision. A husband needs to verbalize love and kindness because that is what his wife longs to hear; it feeds her soul.

Avoid Miscommunication

Don't assume that women are better communicators than men just because they use more words. If you do not speak the same language, it does not matter how many words you use. Miscommunication creates problems in a marriage. One common type of miscommunication occurs when the passive-aggressive spouse will injure the marriage by being sullen and quiet, refusing to communicate. The second type of miscommunication occurs when the hothead will injure the marriage by spouting off hurtful comments in the heat of the moment. When problems occur, husbands and wives

[11] Katherine Paterson, "The Eloquence of 'Silent Cal,'" in *Our White House, Looking In, Looking Out,* by NCBLA, 2008, https://ourwhitehouse.org/the-eloquence-of-silent-cal/.

need to listen and talk with each other so that the problems can be addressed, and solutions can be found.

Be a student of your spouse. Learn how they think and perceive different situations. Learn to verbalize your thoughts in the right way and at the right moment.

Accurate and timely verbalization of thoughts leads to a common understanding. It is the essence of communication and enables teamwork, which leads to intimacy.
The Bible commands husbands to love their wives and commands wives to respect their husbands. Men crave respect, and therefore it is a language that they easily speak and understand; however, women crave love, but that is not a language that comes easily to men. Conversely, women do not easily speak the language of respect, yet that is the language that feeds the souls of men.[12] The Bible teaches us to communicate the emotion that is most needed by our spouse. Husbands, if you respect your wives but do not communicate love, then you do not have a biblical marriage. Wives, if you love your husband but do not communicate respect, then you do not have a biblical marriage.

---

12 For an excellent discussion of this, see Douglas Wilson, "Boy Meets Girl," by Canon Press in "Douglas Wilson on Relationships," October 22, 2020, YouTube video, 56:19.

BIBLICAL *Marriage*

Men, Learn How to Speak to Your Wives

> Husbands, in the same way be considerate as you live with your wives, and treat them with respect as the weaker partner and as heirs with you of the gracious gift of life, so that nothing will hinder your prayers.
> **—1 Peter 3:7 (NIV)**

MEN OFTEN SPEAK harshly to other men without damaging the relationships between them. Coaches are expected to speak harshly to their players. Drill instructors are expected to speak harshly to their recruits. The men on the receiving end of the harsh language are not discouraged by the lack of loving, kind words. They are encouraged to be addressed harshly because it indicates respect; it acknowledges the hardy and resilient nature of the recruit.

Husband, if you are a professional drill instructor, you need to remember that your wife is not one of your recruits. Do not speak to her in the same harsh manner that is appropriate for a recruit. The Bible commands you to respect her weakness. Do you handle a cast-iron skillet in the same way you would handle a delicate piece of fine china? No! That heavy, rugged, cast-iron skillet can take a beating and still serve its purpose, but if you are heavy handed with a fine piece of porcelain china, you will ruin something useful, beautiful, and valuable. Your wife is a precious gift from God. Speak to her accordingly.

Parable of Bill and Jill

One day Bill had a message for his wife. Bill paid someone to encrypt the message. He bought the message even though he did not understand it, for it was encrypted in a language that Bill did not speak. He stopped at a shop on the way home from work and purchased the message. It was a colorful and fragrant message but mysterious beyond comprehension to Bill. When he got home, he placed the message on the table. Jill took one look at the bouquet and understood the message immediately: Bill loves Jill. Bill doesn't understand flowers, but he understands Jill!

Wives, Learn How to Speak to Your Husbands

> For this is the way the holy women of the past who put their hope in God used to make themselves beautiful. They were submissive to their own husbands, like Sarah, who obeyed Abraham and called him her master. You are her daughters if you do what is right and do not give way to fear.
> **—1 Peter 3:5–6 (NIV)**

WIVES, DO NOT speak to your husbands as if you are schoolteachers addressing young students. You might think it is useful to get your way. Your idea might be superior to his, but emasculating your husband is not a desirable solution. If you cannot persuade him with respectful discourse, it

is better to enact his inferior plan than to live with an emasculated husband. Wives, be sure of this: if your husband is manipulated by you, he will be manipulated by many other women. According to the Bible, your husband is your head, even when he is wrong. If you trust God's Word, you should heed God's Word in all circumstances.

Parenting Note

Mothers have the authority to command their children, including their sons; however, when your son reaches puberty, you should change your tone and no longer speak to him as if he were a little boy. He will act like a boy long after the arrival of puberty, but if you persist in addressing him as a child, it will hinder him from embracing manhood. Your condescending words and attitudes will train him to be emasculated by your future daughter-in-law. Speak to him as a young man who will soon be the head of his household, and pray that he will grow into the image that you project upon him.

One More Thing about Communication

Know when to keep your mouth shut. One important form of respect for both husband and wife involves keeping intimate issues within the marriage. Discussions regarding intimate issues should remain between a husband and wife. If concerns arise, they should share details with a Christian marriage counselor when necessary, but intimate details should never be shared with parents, children, or friends. If

Bill talks about his sex life with Jill around the water cooler at work, Jill will feel betrayed. The best way to resolve issues of intimacy between a husband and a wife is to discuss problems between the two of them. This leads to paths of understanding, resolution, and a deeper love!

Questions to Consider

- **Prospective groom: Why is it important for you to understand how to speak to your future wife?**
- **Prospective bride: Why is it important for you to understand how to speak to your future husband?**

CHAPTER 9:
Prayer Matters

Prayer is instant and holy communion with God. Prayer is important to God because he wants to be in a daily relationship with us; therefore, we are commanded to pray.

> Do not be anxious about anything, but in every situation, by prayer and petition, with thanksgiving, present your requests to God.
> **—Philippians 4:6 (NIV)**

Husbands and wives should go to God in prayer about everything so that they are not tempted to worry about anything. We need God's direction to navigate the big and small challenges of married life, so take everything to God in prayer.

We cannot have a biblical marriage apart from prayer as part of our life of faith. We need to pray because alone we are weak, but by spending time in prayer, we are made strong.

> Watch and pray so that you will not fall into temptation. The spirit is willing, but the flesh is weak.
> **—Matthew 26:41, NIV (See also Mark 14:38, Luke 22:46)**

How Husbands Should Pray

A husband should pray for his wife daily. God's Word says, **"He who finds a wife finds what is good and receives favor from the Lord" (Prov. 18:22, NIV).** A husband prays for his wife by thanking God for her. His wife is a good gift from the Lord. Later in the book of Proverbs, God repeats this message: **"A wife of noble character who can find? She is worth far more than rubies" (Prov. 31:10, NIV).** A husband should thank God for his wife.

A husband should pray for unity with his wife, placing her second to God alone **(Mark 10:7–8, Gen. 2:24, Matt. 19:5, Eph. 5:31).** The wife is above all others, including children, parents, extended family, and friends. Praying for unity with his wife will establish and maintain a biblical marriage right from the wedding day.

Husbands are to love their wives as Christ loved the church and gave himself up for her; this type of sacrificial love can only be accomplished through prayer with guidance from the Holy Spirit.

A husband should also pray that the wife of his youth is his only wife. Life, just like feelings, can change, but a marriage is a covenant made before God that is meant to be kept for as long as both the husband and wife are living. A husband should pray for his heart, eyes, and ears to be consistently drawn to his wife and love her completely, no matter the circumstance: **"May your fountain be blessed,**

and may you rejoice in the wife of your youth" (Prov. 5:18, NIV).

Every marriage will be tested through time, but a husband must pray for the devotion to love his wife, no matter the challenge that arises. Jesus explains in the book of Matthew: **"You have heard that it was said, 'You shall not commit adultery.' But I tell you that anyone who looks at a woman lustfully has already committed adultery with her in his heart" (Matt. 5:27–28, NIV).** A husband should pray for daily strength to resist any temptation to look away from his wife and in the direction of another woman on television, on the internet, or in real life.

A husband should also pray for his wife so he can faithfully demonstrate confidence in her: **"Her husband has full confidence in her and lacks nothing of value" (Prov. 31:11, NIV).** A husband should look for opportunities to voice his confidence in his wife through words and actions: **"Her children arise and call her blessed; her husband also, and he praises her" (Prov. 31:28, NIV).**

> **A husband should praise and encourage his wife as a way of demonstrating respect for her and love for her.**

A HUSBAND SHOULD pray for guidance as he leads his wife and children in a way that honors the Lord. The husband needs the wisdom of God to lead in righteousness.

How Wives Should Pray

A wife should pray daily for her husband and for spiritual unity with her husband. Part of praying for spiritual unity begins with the importance of leaving and cleaving.

A wife must leave her parents, family, and home before there can be a biblical marriage. A wife should pray for wisdom to place her husband second to God alone, above all others, including children, parents, and friends.

A noble wife in a biblical marriage will treat her husband with respect: **"Her husband is respected at the city gate, where he takes his seat among the elders of the land" (Prov. 31:23, NIV).** The wife should pray for the Holy Spirit to lead her in the ways she is to respect her husband.

How Couples Should Pray

Marriages without consistent prayer will be more likely to encounter hardship and difficulties. A strong prayer life for our spouses and with our spouses is not optional; instead, it is a command for our benefit. Any time we pray is time well spent: **"The Lord is far from the wicked, but he hears the prayer of the righteous" (Prov. 15:29, NIV).** Therefore, we should take our requests to God, believing that we will receive what we ask of him.

Couples should spend time together in prayer every day praying for God's guidance in the marriage. Prayer has the power to quicken (bring to life) the relationship between husband and wife, which may have grown cold. Pray, and

have faith in those prayers. Let us come boldly before the throne of grace for direction, clarity, and encouragement to live out our life of faith with our spouses in the marriages that God has created for us. God's Word tells us the following: **"The prayer of a righteous person is powerful and effective" (James 5:16, NIV); "If you believe, you will receive whatever you ask for in prayer" (Matt. 21:22, NIV);** and **"Therefore I tell you, whatever you ask for in prayer, believe that you have received it, and it will be yours" (Mark 11:24, NIV).**

> Prayer is not just a tool for life; it gives life. Prayer is just like anything else in this life; we must use it for it to work.

TO LIVE A life in our strength requires little or no dependence on God, but for husbands and wives who want biblical marriages, these things are impossible apart from prayer. Prayer is sacred to God and should therefore be sacred to a husband and a wife who desire a biblical marriage: **"And this is my prayer: that your love may abound more and more in knowledge and depth of insight" (Phil. 1:9, NIV).** Biblical marriages will have a love that continues to grow just by spending time in prayer.

> Marriages held together by prayer are not quickly unraveled.

Questions to Consider

- Do you pray for each other now?
- What are some specific ways in which you can pray for your husband or wife?

CHAPTER 10:
Money Matters

When we got married, my pastor began our marriage counseling by walking us through what he considered to be **the three main causes of conflict in marriage: issues involving family, issues involving sex, and issues involving money.** Now those reasons may surprise you, but the statistics bear this out. Money and financial wealth expert Dave Ramsey writes, "Money fights are the second leading cause of divorce, behind infidelity."[13]

Money is an obvious issue that causes conflict within many marriages. While there are many solutions that people have offered to rectify these issues, rarely do we find much thought as to what God would say about how a couple should view money. This chapter will seek to provide some basic principles that God reveals in his Word about money and marriage. God's Word is sufficient to address every issue in marriage including this one.

Parable of Bill and Jill

Before marriage, Bill and Jill were used to living alone. Bill has his bank account, and Jill has hers. They've both paid their own

[13] Dave Ramsey, "Money, Marriage, and Communication: The Link Between Relationship Problems and Finances," Online Article, https://www.ramseysolutions.com/relationships/money-marriage-communication-research.

bills. They bought their own cars, and they have successfully lived independent lives.

So upon getting married, they decide to keep it all the same. Jill had the nicer home, so Bill will move in with her and sell his home, and he will take over some of the bills that Jill had, but they agree that they will keep their accounts separate.

But Jill has a spending problem. She likes to shop. Better put, she likes to buy. Before long, Jill has racked up a hefty credit card bill from online shopping. So she goes to Bill and tells him that she will not be able to afford to pay the electrical bill this month. Bill gets angry. "Why not?" he says. She explains to him that she had overspent, but Bill cannot understand how she could be so irresponsible. On top of that, he had been saving money for over a year to buy a new set of golf clubs, and he had recently saved just enough to do so. Bill was a strict budgeter, but he was not expecting to have this new bill thrown in his lap.

As a result, Bill and Jill argue about Jill's spending habits. Jill does not see why it's a big deal for him to have to pay this one month. Bill is upset that Jill has selfishly just thrown this on him. Both are angry at each other.

They argue about this, but Bill ends up paying to avoid having the lights shut off in their home. But he resents her for this. He will have to wait to buy his golf clubs for a few more months now. In his mind, that was his money, not hers. That was her bill to pay, not his, and now there is a strain in their marriage.

Because We Are One

The Bible repeatedly explains an important theological truth regarding marriage. When a man unites with a woman in marriage, they become one flesh. They become one unit. The very first expression of marriage is reflected in Genesis 2:24, where God said this:

> For this reason a man shall leave his father and his mother, and be joined to his wife; and they shall become one flesh.(NASB)

Later Jesus will repeat this same principle in Mark 10:7–9:

> FOR THIS REASON A MAN SHALL LEAVE HIS FATHER AND MOTHER, AND THE TWO SHALL BECOME ONE FLESH; so they are no longer two, but one flesh. "What therefore God has joined together, let no man separate.(NASB)

This principle found in these two passages and many others is clear: when two people are married, they become one. The two become a single unit that lives together in that regard. They are no longer separate according to God.

However, many families unite in almost every way *except* when it comes to money. The husband has his own separate bank account, and the wife has her own separate bank account. They split the bills; one will pay some bills, and the other will take the bills left over. Then they spend their money on what they individually desire with "their own" money.

Some say that this is a safeguard against fighting about money. They believe that because their money is separate, they are less likely to fight over money. That belief is naive, and it is my opinion that this practice is altogether unbiblical when we look at the language of marriage in the Bible.

According to God's Word, as we have already stated when you marry, you become one. In other words, you are no longer two individuals, but rather, you are now a collective unit. This theological truth, I believe, will help solve many of the woes of couples struggling financially.

This means that what is the husband's is now the wife's, and vice versa. Because of this biblical truth, we have sought to live this out in our marriage. Therefore, when we got married, my money and my debts were now hers, and her money and her debts were now mine. When we talk about money, we do not speak in terms of *my money* and *her money*. We speak about *our money* because we are one. We share a bank account. What we purchase, we purchase together with both of our names listed on the title. When we file our taxes, we file together. When we face financial trouble, we face it together. Likewise, when we have financial successes, we enjoy them together. We do not mention whether or not one makes more than the other. What we make, we make together. We are one.

This also means that there is to be no hiding and no underhandedness whatsoever. We work together for the good of each other because we are one.

The moment we begin to think of money or anything we have as "mine" or "theirs," we have missed the mark of what God desires our marriages to be. We are trying to divide what God has united. This was Bill and Jill's problem.

This principle of togetherness guards against temptations that we may have. One temptation that may arise in this aspect of marriage is to have an "escape plan." I have seen this occur many times, where a spouse who makes more money than the other will lay money aside just in case he or she needs to escape the marriage. The reality here is that this kind of mindset is worldly wisdom and not godly wisdom.

To have an "escape plan" is to already have one foot out the door. There is no "escape plan." In your marriage vows, you made a covenant where you vowed to be together "for better, for worse…till death do us part." Therefore, death is the only reason the unity of the marriage might be severed. Until you die, you are one, and to have an "escape plan" is to divide yourselves unnecessarily. In reality, to lay aside "your money" is to be unfaithful to your spouse. It is not "your money" as an individual. It is your money together.

I have had conversations with struggling couples who held separate accounts. Their attitude was that they could do just fine without the other. They were content to live and take care of themselves. This attitude sprang forth from having separate accounts, having separate bills, and essentially living as two separate individuals within the same home. As a result, both developed a mindset in which they knew they could take care of themselves, and they weaponized that information against their spouse.

Again, this is not what God intended. God intended couples to be unified in every aspect of their lives, including money.

I know the tendency may be to disregard this chapter as unimportant, outdated, or just not a big deal, but from experience, I can assure you that being unified about financial matters is a wonderful thing. It is a safeguard for unity, and it is a critical step toward a biblical marriage and a peaceful home.

If you are struggling financially, please take time to read some good books on this subject. Dave Ramsey says the book of Proverbs is the greatest book on financial advice ever written. Dave Ramsey has also written many excellent books (and YouTube videos) on the subject.

BIBLICAL *Marriage*

Questions to Consider

- What will you do with your money when you get married?
- What are your current debts and financial accounts? What financial information does your spouse need to know?
- What will your financial budget look like once you are a married couple?

CHAPTER 11:
Church Matters

Both the husband and the wife must be committed to a local church where they *both* worship, serve, and attend regularly because this is necessary for Christians to thrive in a relationship with Christ.

The Biblical Reason for Church Attendance

Church attendance is a matter of obedience to God. Some people have wrongly assumed that church attendance is an option to be considered rather than a response to a clearly defined command in Scripture. This assumption could not be further from reality. God has commanded believers to gather together regularly. He did so in Hebrews 10:23–25:

> Let us hold fast the confession of our hope without wavering, for He who promised is faithful; and let us consider how to stimulate one another to love and good deeds, not forsaking our own assembling together, as is the habit of some, but encouraging one another; and all the more as you see the day drawing near.(NASB)

The author of Hebrews, inspired by God, writes to a group of Christians and commands them to not forsake gathering together. In verse 23 of chapter 10, he first encourages them to hold fast to the confession of their hope without wavering. In other words, he wants them to remain faithful to the Lord. Secondly, he urges them to stimulate one another to do good deeds. Finally, he adds this command of not forsaking the assembling of themselves together. He adds this final command because it would be impossible to accomplish the first two commands without actually being involved and committed to a local church.

One of the means by which we remain faithful to our confession of Jesus is through constant encouragement by a group of confessing Christians in the context of a local church. How we stimulate one another toward love and good deeds is by regularly meeting together with other believers. Once again, you will find that encouragement in a local church.

So he commands us: "Don't *forsake* the assembling of ourselves together." That word *forsake* could be translated this way: **let there be no lack** of gathering together. In other words, don't leave it behind for anything. Don't abandon it for anything. Don't desert it for anything. Let there be no lack.

We live in a world today where this mindset is altogether absent. People find every reason not to go to church rather than prioritizing church attendance over and above everything else. This is no small matter. Church attendance is a matter of obedience. God has commanded it!

So what is it when we do forsake the assembling of ourselves together? Put simply, it is disobedience. It is sin because we are either ignoring or willfully disobeying God. I do realize there are, at times, *legitimate* issues in life that prevent us from gathering as a whole and as individuals. But most of the time, it boils down to two things: a lack of prioritization or a lack of effort. Either something else is more fun or more important to us than the worship of God, or in our laziness, we simply choose sloth over worship.

I cannot overstate the importance of this. You must devote yourselves to the local church if you desire your walk with Christ to grow and flourish, and you must devote yourselves to a local church if you want your marriage to flourish as Christ intended.

Typical Questions You Might Have

Q: Is it sufficient for me and my family just to join in worshipping from home? Do I have to go to church? Or can I just worship from home now?

A: The short answer is *no*, and there are some biblical reasons and also some very practical reasons why merely joining online is not sufficient. The author of Hebrews in Hebrews 10:25 commands us to "not forsake the ASSEMBLING of ourselves TOGETHER (NASB Emphasis Mine)." The simple reading of this text is that we are to assemble regularly with other Christians in our local church to encourage one another to stand firm and to encourage each toward obeying God's will. Neither one of those things happen if people stay home and just watch online.

Many other reasons exist, including but not limited to the following:

- While watching online, you cannot join in with singing the truths of the faith with others inside your church.
- You cannot participate in corporate times of prayer.
- You cannot encourage those who may be struggling in their faith while you watch at home.
- You cannot be there to be a shoulder to cry on or a listening ear to others who may have just received a critical diagnosis or may have even lost a loved one.
- You cannot enjoy the full benefits of brotherly and sisterly accountability while at home.
- You cannot participate in the Lord's Supper or be present for the baptism of other members while at home.

Practically speaking, "just watching online" is also problematic. During the COVID-19 pandemic, our church went to online services for a brief time when several within our church family tested positive for the virus. This was during a time when we were still uncertain as to the deadliness of the virus and the uncertainty of how contagious it was.

During this time, I would prerecord my sermon and upload it to our streaming service to prevent any technical difficulties when it came time for service on Sunday. However, at times, there were still technical difficulties: the microphone would stop working, the video would time out, the internet would run slowly, and it was hard to stay on track because we were constantly waiting for the video to buffer. None of these challenges are present when we are physically present.

During this time, there was something about being at home watching the service online that was less serious, less sacred, and quite frankly, less profitable. We all watched in the clothes we had worn the night before. There was little to no preparation for worship. Our children were more concerned with playing with their toys than with listening to the sermon. At one point, we were in the middle of watching the sermon, and we received a knock at our door; we felt compelled to answer it. All in all, it seemed like it was just another day rather than a day set aside for the Lord.

Q: Why do I need to go to Sunday School or attend a small group?

A: Over the past few years, many have decided that they will only attend the main worship gathering in the church. The worship gathering is important for families, but I also want to stress the importance of being involved in Sunday School or small group meetings throughout the week.

Sunday School or small groups are the intimate settings in which we can help others, and they can help us in our walk with Christ. In most worship services, the format is such that there is little time given for interaction. Small groups and Sunday School are designed to be more intimate. It is in these small group settings that we have opportunities to share struggles and prayer requests and ask questions regarding the Bible, theology, or practical matters involving the Christian life.

In addition, attending a small group or Bible study with other Christians of the same gender is profitable as well. Males and females have different struggles, different experiences, and different questions. Because God has designed males and females with different roles within the home and in the church, gathering together in a more intimate setting with people of the same gender can provide more liberty to ask questions or to speak about your struggles.

To put it simply, attending both small groups and worship services is profitable for believers if they desire to grow in their walk with Christ.

Q: What role should worship play in my home?

A: Sunday morning worship services are not the only times you and your family should be worshipping God. Family worship is vital to the spiritual growth of the family. We find this principle in Scripture as well. In Deuteronomy 6, Moses is addressing the people of Israel about the need for their homes to be constantly centered around the worship of God:

> Hear, O Israel! The LORD is our God, the LORD is one! You shall love the LORD your God with all your heart and with all your soul and with all your might. These words, which I am commanding you today, shall be on your heart. You shall teach them diligently to your sons and shall talk of them when you sit in your house and when you walk by the way and when you lie down and when you rise up. You shall bind them as a sign on your hand and they shall be as frontals on your forehead. You shall write them on the doorposts of your house and on your gates.
>
> **(Deut. 6:4–9, NASB)**

IN THIS PASSAGE, we learn that the love and worship of God should permeate every aspect of our lives. The words of God are "to be on our heart." We are to "teach them diligently" to our children. We are to speak of God's word "when you sit in your house and when you walk by the way and when you lie down and when you rise up." In other words, we are to teach our children the Word of God diligently, using every opportunity we are given to speak the truth and life of Scripture.

Our family spends time daily with our three girls reading the Bible, praying, and teaching them basic Bible doctrine using a question-and-answer book that deals with basic theological topics. During these times, our girls ask questions, and we discuss their questions together as a family. These are some of the sweetest times with my girls as they wrestle with the truths of the Christian faith. My prayer is that one day, God will use these times in his Word to soften their hearts and draw them to faith in Christ Jesus.

Finally, the word of God is to be ever present in front of us, evidenced by the command to "write them on the doorposts of your house and on your gates." There is a reason for the imagery of the doorposts and the gates having God's Word written there. This means more than literally writing Scripture on every wall and door in your house. This means that our homes are to be guarded and guided by God's Word. We decide what kinds of things we will allow into our homes and lives, having been informed by God's Word, and we must guard our homes against the things God forbids in his Word. Additionally, when we decide on the direction of our homes, the Word of God is to be our guide. The decisions we make are to be filtered through God's perfect Word.

Final Thoughts: Picking a Church

Once again, I cannot overstate the need for you to entrench your lives in a strong, biblical, local church. This will be key to maintaining a healthy marriage at home.

When you are picking a church, there are a few questions to ask:

- **What does the church believe?**

Before you join a church, you need to look at the doctrinal statement of the church. Find out what the church confesses to believe, and test those beliefs with God's Word. Find out if the church's doctrine is biblical.

- **Does the pastor preach God's Word?**
  Whenever you listen to him preach, does he tell you what the Bible says, or does he use the Bible to say what he wants to say? There is a difference. I suggest finding a church and a pastor who systematically preaches through books of the Bible regularly.

- **Will I be held accountable?**
  Some churches would be easy to choose because they have little accountability. Some churches are structured in ways that you could easily miss several Sundays without anyone ever having missed you being there. Find a church that will hold you accountable. Find a church that will miss you when you are not there.

- **How can I serve here?**
  Too many people ask the opposite question. Many will ask: "How can I be served here?" Join a church that needs you to serve. Join a church where there will be many opportunities to serve both within the church and within the community surrounding the church.

- **Why am I joining this church?**

So many people join churches for the wrong reasons such as: proximity to home, the size of the church, or preferential matters like music or programs offered, or they just keep going to the place where they were raised. It's not that those things are always bad. It could be that you were raised in a strong, biblical church that checks all the boxes above, and that is where you will flourish most as a family to the glory of God. If that is the case, then praise God! Go, and go often! However, we need to be honest enough to ask ourselves why we are joining the church we are joining.

THE MAIN REASON we join a church is to unite ourselves with a like-minded body of believers with whom we can grow and serve God for his glory and our good.

Once you choose a church, commit your life to it. Don't just leave the first time your feelings are hurt or the first time you may not get your way. When you unite to a church, unite to it as your church family. Love the people there, bear with the people there, and serve the people there to the glory of God.

CHAPTER 12:
Conclusion

Relationships are difficult, but they are worthwhile. Marriage is the most important human relationship that God has gifted to us. It requires a great deal of work, but the value of a good marriage is extraordinary. If you follow the Bible's recipe for marriage, you will enjoy the greatest, most intimate relationship possible. When you veer off course of the biblical path, you do so at your peril. Sin has consequences.

As believers, we should desire that our marriages be the picture of the Gospel that God intended them to be.

To be clear, this is the Gospel. Jesus Christ, the only perfect husband, came to the earth, born of a virgin. He lived a perfectly sinless life. He was crucified at the hands of godless men. On the cross, Jesus became sin for us. God the Father punished Jesus in our place. He died on that cross, but he rose again three days later victorious. He ascended into heaven, and one day, he is coming back. The Husband sacrificially laid down his life for his bride, and one day he is coming back to get her to take her home and to a grand marriage supper.

Until he does come back, we have marriage to be a picture of Christ's relationship with his church. Also, we have been commanded to share that message with the world and call them to repent and turn to Christ, who can give them eternal life and true purpose in this life.

ABOUT THE AUTHORS

BENJAMIN HUTSON received his Doctor of Ministry from Southeastern Baptist Theological Seminary in 2021. Benjamin currently serves as the pastor of Mt. Pisgah Baptist Church in Nichols, South Carolina where he has recently completed his 7th year of ministry as the pastor.

LAUREN HUTSON received her Bachelor's degree in Nursing from Francis Marion University. Lauren is a stay-at-home mother while working part-time at a local hospital where she works as a Certified Lactation Consultant and a Registered Nurse. Benjamin and Lauren have three girls: Abigail, Evan-Grace, and Anna-Claire.

MANDY VIPPERMAN received her Bachelor's degree in both English and Education in 1994 from UNC-G. She earned her Master's degree in 1997 from Regent University and her Ed.D. in Educational Leadership from Liberty University in 2021. She is currently teaching at Myrtle Beach High School and serves as an Adjunct Professor to doctoral candidates at Liberty University.

STEPHEN VIPPERMAN graduated from The Citadel in 1993 and Southwestern Baptist Theological Seminary in 2000. In between, he served four years with SEAL Team

FOUR. Stephen pastored Bear Swamp Baptist Church, Lake View, SC from 2000-2014 and is currently pastor of Mount Olive Baptist Church, Horry County, SC. Stephen and Mandy began dating in high school and married in 1994. Together they have two beautiful children, Anna and Jason.

www.ingramcontent.com/pod-product-compliance
Lightning Source LLC
LaVergne TN
LVHW012030060526
838201LV00061B/4543